DORRIE and the Haunted House

Written and illustrated by
Patricia Coombs

A YEARLING BOOK

Published by
Dell Publishing Co., Inc.
1 Dag Hammarskjold Plaza
New York, New York 10017

Yearling ® TM 913705, Dell Publishing Co., Inc.

ISBN: 0-440-42212-4

Reprinted by arrangement with Lothrop, Lee and Shepard Co.

Printed in the United States of America
Fifth printing—November 1984

FL

For my mother

Dorrie is a witch. A little witch. Her hat is always on crooked. Her socks don't match and her hair isn't combed. She lives in a house with a tall, tall tower. Inside the tower is a little secret room where the Big Witch mixes up magic.

One day, just before Halloween, the sky grew dark and the wind began to blow. Dorrie and her black cat Gink were looking out the window.

"Look at all the Witches and Wizards!" said Dorrie. "They're coming to our house! Come on, Gink, something has gone wrong."

Down, down, down the stairs went Dorrie, and so did Gink.

Witches and Wizards in all shapes and sizes were crowded into the hall. They were all talking at once.

"Shhhh!" cried the Big Witch. "Squig, tell me what is wrong."

Squig waved his umbrella and shouted, "Uncle King Dimly and Mad Mac stole the Blue Ruby from the Town Power Tower. We forgot to renew the spell that banishes bandits!

If we don't get the Blue Ruby back by four o'clock, Dimley will have the power to turn us into weathervanes—and toads—and park benches!"

The clock struck two. The Big Witch frowned.

"They went into the woods near here," said Mr. Obs. "But with the Blue Ruby gone from the tower, our crystal balls won't work, so we don't know where they are hiding."

"Quick!" said the Big Witch. "Up to the secret room. We will mix a batch of my famous glue spell. With all the doors and windows glued shut, Dimly won't be able to get in here. Then we will mix a potion so strong that when I dip my fingers in it, I can lead us to the Blue Ruby. We must hurry if we are to find the Blue Ruby by four o'clock!"

All the Witches and Wizards flocked up the stairs toward the secret room while the Big Witch mumbled over her plan.

Dorrie and Gink were right behind her. "I'll help," said Dorrie. "I can do the stirring."

"NO!" said the Big Witch. "Go back downstairs and wait. This is the most IMPORTANT MAGIC ever mixed. It is only for grown-ups. You must be very good and very *quiet.*"

With a swirl and swish of her long black gown
the Big Witch vanished up the stairs into the tower.

Dorrie sighed. Down, down, down the stairs she
went, and Gink went with her.

Dorrie thought and thought. "I know, Gink," she said, "We'll draw a face on the pumpkin. Drawing is nice and quiet. Come on, it's right outside the door."

Dorrie and Gink went outside to get the pumpkin. It was raining and the wind was blowing harder and harder. The door slammed shut behind them.

Dorrie picked up the pumpkin. She tried to open
the door. It wouldn't open. She tried and tried.

Orange and purple sparks swirled down with the
rain. "Oh, no!" said Dorrie, "That's the glue spell!
Mother just glued us out of the house."

The rain was coming down harder and harder.
"We can't stay here, Gink," said Dorrie. "We'll
run over to Mr. Obs's house and wait on his porch."
Down the hill and into the woods they ran.

They ran and ran and ran. Along one path, then another, and another. It was getting darker all the time, and raining so hard they could barely see. They got wetter and wetter.

Suddenly they saw a big gray house looming between the trees.

There was a crash of thunder and a flash of lightning. They ran up the broken steps to the old porch.

Broken shutters banged in the wind. Vines and branches skreeked against the house.

"Wow!" said Dorrie. "We took the wrong path. This isn't Mr. Obs's house. I never saw this place before. It will keep us dry, anyway. Come on, Gink."

Dorrie gave the door a push. It creaked open and they stepped inside. Dorrie squeezed the rain out of her hat and shoes. Gink shook himself.

"It sure is dark and spooky in here," said Dorrie, peering through a doorway. "I bet it's haunted. I bet we found the ghost house Mother used to talk about. Come on, Gink, let's explore."

Dorrie tiptoed into the parlor and Gink went with her. Mice scurried away into corners. Bats flapped past her hat. Old dusty curtains hung like ragged ghosts at the dark windows. Wind whistled in the black, empty chimney.

Dorrie and Gink tiptoed around piles of books and boxes and old furniture covered with dust and cobwebs.

Outside, branches scritched and skreeked louder and louder against the house. Lightning flashed and thunder boomed. Dorrie jumped. Gink's fur stood on end. There were rattles and crashes and thumps.

"This storm," said Dorrie, "is making a lot of racket. It almost sounds as if somebody is in the house besides us."

They tiptoed into the old dining room and looked around. Mice had made nests in the chair cushions, and cobwebs hung over everything.

"Oh, goody," whispered Dorrie, as the cobwebs fluttered and swayed in the dark air. "I'm glad we got glued out of the house. This is better than stirring stuff in a smelly old cauldron in a stuffy old tower."

Dorrie found another door and pushed it open. "Look, Gink, a haunted kitchen," she whispered. "If Cook saw this she'd have a fit of grumbles for a month."

Vines had grown through a crack in the window. Rusty kettles and pots, bottles and pans and cans, dishes and bowls and ladles and spoons were scattered all over.

Rain spattered against the window. Lightning flashed brighter and brighter. Bats flapped and squeaked. A crash of thunder shook the house until it rattled. There were thuds and bumps and a strange whispering sound.

"It's getting spookier around here all the time," said Dorrie. "Let's go down that hall. Maybe there's a pantry like the one at home."

Down the dark hall they went. They came to a small door. Dorrie grabbed the rusty handle and turned it. The door slowly squeaked open and they went inside.

A glimmer of light from a narrow window shone on shelves of dusty jars and jugs, on bins and brooms and a big flour barrel left near the window.

"It is the pantry, and it really is scary," said Dorrie. "There's so much dust on the pickle jars they look like ghost pick——" Dorrie stopped. A flash of lightning brightened the room; and in the dust and flour around the barrel there were footprints. Great BIG footprints.

Lightning flashed again. Thunder rolled and boomed and the house shook. The pantry door swung shut behind them.

"Oh, oh! Ghosts! Listen, Gink!" whispered Dorrie. It wasn't branches skreeking and shutters banging in the wind. The sounds were coming from *inside* the house. Footsteps and voices were coming closer and CLOSER and CLOSER.

Dorrie ran to the window. She scrambled up on a stool and tried to open the window. It wouldn't open. She pushed harder.

Suddenly the stool skidded and Dorrie fell down, down, down right into the old flour barrel. And so did Gink.

Heavy footsteps creaked, then stopped outside the pantry door. Voices argued back and forth, louder and louder.

Dorrie held Gink and wiggled down into the flour as far as she could.

"Ouch! I sat on something sharp. It feels like a rock," whispered Dorrie, reaching down into the flour. She shoved it into her pocket and held Gink closer.

Lightning flashed. Gink sneezed. Thunder crashed. Dorrie sneezed.

"It's the flour," said Dorrie. She sneezed again. "Those ghosts will find us for sure if we keep sneezing. Come on."

They scrambled out of the barrel, all white with the flour, and hid in a dark corner near the door.

The voices stopped. Slowly, with a loud creak, the door was pushed open. A great big shadowy shape and a smaller one crept into the pantry and over toward the flour barrel.

A clap of thunder shook the house. Dorrie grabbed Gink and dashed out of the pantry and slammed the door. It slammed so hard the rusty handle fell on the floor.

Dorrie raced to the front door. It was locked. Voices from the pantry were yelling LOUDER and LOUDER, and they sounded MADDER and MAD-DER.

"A ghost! I saw it. A ghost took the Ruby!"
"Stupid! It's a trick. You're seeing things!"
"I am not!" Thud.
"You are so!" Crash.
"Help! The ghost locked the door and took the Ruby. Dimly, we're trapped!"

Dorrie didn't wait to hear any more. She whirled around and raced upstairs with Gink. She dashed into a room and slammed the door and locked it.

Dorrie put Gink down and looked around. "It's an old bathroom. Those ghosts are so busy arguing about some other ghost, maybe they won't look for us."

Dorrie listened. The banging and crashing had stopped. She heard footsteps running around and around, doors being opened, boxes sliding, and once in a while a shout.

"Oh, help, they're after us!" said Dorrie. She jumped into the old bathtub with Gink and pulled a rug over them.

"It's awfully dark," she whispered to Gink. "Maybe they won't look for us in here. Maybe it will be too dark for them to see us."

They hid under the rug and listened. They listened and listened. All they could hear was the rain and branches skreeking in the wind.

All at once there was a whooshing, spinning sound. It grew very, very quiet, and even darker. There was another whoosh and the sound of voices far away, then closer and closer.

Footsteps came creaking up, up, up the stairs and down the hall.

They stopped outside the door.

"Oh, Gink," whispered Dorrie, "the ghosts have found us!"

The handle of the door rattled. It was wiggling to and fro with a scritching sound.

Dorrie sat up. "GO AWAY!" yelled Dorrie. "You can't come in. I'm taking a bath. And so is my cat."

A voice called out, "Dorrie, is that you? Open the door!"

It was the Big Witch! Dorrie jumped out of the tub and flung open the door.

The Big Witch and all the other Witches and Wizards were crowded around. They took one look at Dorrie, and yelling and shouting, "HELP! GHO-O-O-OSTS!" they all scurried down, down, down the stairs. Out of the house and into the woods they went.

Dorrie and Gink ran after them.

Through the woods they ran. Suddenly, as they came near Dorrie's house, there was a shout from behind some trees.

And the two shapes from the haunted house ran after the Witches and Wizards and slipped into the house right behind them. The door slammed and locked.

"Oh, my!" said Dorrie. "Now those ghosts are inside OUR house. Maybe Mother found the Ruby and the ghosts are trying to take it away. We've got to warn her, Gink."

Sparks were shooting out of the tower and whirling in the wind and rain, around and around. There were great puffs of purple smoke.

Dorrie stood in the yard with Gink and yelled up at the tower. She yelled and yelled.

At last the Big Witch poked her head out and looked down. Dorrie and Gink were standing in the rain with the flour dripping off them. Dorrie's clothes and Gink were slowly turning black again.

"It's Dorrie!" shouted the Big Witch. "Not a ghost at all." There was a flash of magic from the tower and a rainbow of sparks. The front door swung open.

Dorrie and Gink ran inside as fast as they could go. They ran smack into the great big shadowy shape and the smaller shadowy shape. The shapes banged heads, and they landed in a heap on the hall floor.

Just then the Big Witch and all the other Witches and Wizards came rushing down the stairs.

"LOOK!" cried the Big Witch. "Dorrie has knocked out Uncle King Dimly and Mad Mac! We're saved!"

Dorrie looked at the heap of bandits. The Witches and Wizards were looking through the bandits' pockets for the Blue Ruby.

"I thought they were *ghosts,*" said Dorrie. "They chased us all over the place. I was scared. And so was Gink." Dorrie frowned. "If I were a big witch I'd point at them, whirl around three times and say: VANISH, BANDITS, BANISHED BE!"

As Dorrie said that the heap on the floor vanished into the air, and a cloud of orange and pink and purple sparks floated out of her pocket.

"Dorrie! You have the power to banish! You found the Blue Ruby. No wonder the bandits were chasing you," cried the Big Witch.

"Me?" said Dorrie. "I didn't find anything. Just an old rock. It was in the flour barrel and Gink and I sat on it." Dorrie showed it to the Big Witch.

The Big Witch rubbed the flour and rain off the Blue Ruby and held it up for everyone to see.

It shone in every shade of orange and red and blue and pink and purple. It glowed like a small strange moon in the Big Witch's hand. Just then the clock struck four.

"HURRAH!" they all shouted.

And they ran out of the house, chanting a spell to end the wind and rain. Then they marched in a long parade into town to put the Blue Ruby back safely in the Town Tower.

Mr. Obs played his violin and they all sang songs. Squig turned Dinger's hat into tin and gave it to Dorrie to bang on as a drum.

They paraded back to Dorrie's house and told ghost stories until very, very late.

The stories were so scary the Witches and Wizards were afraid to go home in the dark, so they all spent the night in the parlor.

Cook mixed up hundreds of pancakes with purple syrup for breakfast. All the Wizards and Witches voted to make that day a special holiday ever after. They would call it Dorriesday.

"Gink helped," said Dorrie. "He fell into the flour barrel on top of the Blue Ruby, too."

So they all voted to have a Ginksarade every year on Dorriesday. Every year they'd renew the banish-bandit spell and tell ghost stories and eat pancakes with purple syrup.

And they did.

DORRIE

PATRICIA COOMBS

Dorrie, the spirited apprentice witch, is lovable and lively as she outwits some bad bigger witches in these six tales of wit and witchery.

____DORRIE AND THE AMAZING
    MAGIC ELIXIR........................$1.95 (41684-1)
____DORRIE AND THE BLUE WITCH $2.50 (42210-8)
____DORRIE AND THE DREAMYARD
    MONSTERS.........................$1.95 (40896-2)
____DORRIE AND THE HALLOWEEN PLOT $2.25 (42076-8)
____DORRIE AND THE HAUNTED HOUSE......$2.25 (42212-4)
____DORRIE AND THE WITCH'S IMP..........$1.75 (40889-X)

YEARLING BOOKS